G000229330

Cover illustration: The scene from the bridge of HMS *Euryalus* showing Vian's flagship *Cleopatra* laying the smokescreen which hid Convoy MW.10 from the Italians, March 1942. See photographs 35–44. (IWM A.8166)

Back cover, top: HMS *Welshman* made a fourth supply run to the island in November 1942; the photograph shows her approaching her berth in Grand Harbour on the 18th. The wreck in the foreground is that of the oiler *Plumleaf*. (IWM A.13063)

Back cover, bottom: Was all the effort and sacrifice to maintain Malta worthwhile? An Italian merchant ship loaded with supplies for the Axis forces in North Africa and seen here sinking after an attack by Malta-based aircraft expresses the vital role played by the island in the war in the Mediterranean. The submarines, ships and aircraft based on Malta made an enormous contribution to British victories in the Western Desert by depriving the Axis forces of vital supplies. (IWM C.1913)

1. A well-known photograph taken from the after end of the carrier *Victorious'* flight deck during Operation 'Pedestal' in August 1942 and showing *Indomitable* leading *Eagle*. A Sea Hurricane and an Albacore are ranged on *Victorious'* flight deck. (IWM A.11293)

Malta Convoys
1940-1943

PAUL J. KEMP

a&
ap

ARMS & ARMOUR PRESS

London   New York   Sydney

Introduction

First published in Great Britain in 1988 by Arms & Armour Press Ltd., Artillery House, Artillery Row, London SW1P 1RT.

Distributed in the USA by Sterling Publishing Co. Inc., 2 Park Avenue, New York, NY 10016.

Distributed in Australia by Capricorn Link (Australia) Pty. Ltd., P.O. Box 665, Lane Cove, New South Wales 2066.

British Library Cataloguing in Publication data:
Kemp, Paul.
Malta convoys, 1940–1943. —
(Warships illustrated; no. 14).
1. Malta. Convoys from Great Britain: 1939–1945
I. Title   II. Series
940.54′5941

ISBN 0-85368-922-9

Edited and designed by Roger Chesneau.
Typeset by Typesetters (Birmingham) Ltd.
Printed and bound in Great Britain by
The Bath Press.

Prints credited to the Imperial War Museum (IWM) are available on application to the Department of Photographs, Lambeth Road, London, SE1. The Visitors' Room is open to the public by appointment.

The passage of a convoy through narrow waters in the face of determined opposition by enemy naval and air forces is one of the most hazardous seaborne operations that can be undertaken. Nowhere was this more true than in the British efforts to supply the island of Malta and to maintain the naval and air forces based there during the Second World War.

Yet Malta barely figured in British prewar planning, for both the War Office and the Air Ministry considered that the island was untenable since it lay within 30 minutes' flying time from Italian airfields in Sicily. Only the Admiralty advocated the role that Malta could play as a base for forces to block Axis supply lines to North Africa. Fortunately Winston Churchill agreed, and the decision was made that it must be held.

Since Malta was not self-supporting, the island had to be supplied by sea by convoys of heavily escorted merchant ships sailing either from Gibraltar or from Alexandria. They endured every form of attack imaginable, and heavy losses were suffered among the escorts and merchant ships alike. The convoy battles culminated in the summer of 1942 in the famous 'Pedestal' operation and the epic voyage of the tanker *Ohio*.

However, convoys were not the only means by which Malta was supplied. Submarines were used to take urgently needed items as well as unorthodox cargoes such as aviation fuel. The fast minelayers HMS *Welshman* and *Manxman* were also employed to supply Malta, their phenomenally high speeds enabling them to make the voyage from Gibraltar or Alexandria unescorted.

Was the struggle to maintain Malta worth the effort when the forces required to escort these convoys were in such demand in other theatres of war? The role played by the ships, aircraft and submarines based in Malta in the disruption of Axis supply lines to North Africa cannot be overemphasized. If Malta had fallen, then not only would communications with the Middle East and control of the central Mediterranean have been lost but the reconquest of North Africa would have taken immeasurably longer.

The story of the Malta convoys is the story of one of the great naval campaigns of the Second World War. The convoys were fought through to the island often against overwhelming odds. The courage and tenacity of their naval escorts is undeniable, but perhaps the last word should go to the men of the merchant ships, of whom Vice-Admiral Syfret said, 'The memory of their conduct will remain an inspiration to all who were privileged to sail with them'.

The majority of the photographs in this volume come from the extensive collection of the Imperial War Museum, and I am grateful to that institution for permission to reproduce them. Grateful thanks are also due to Julie Fulcher for her assistance with the preparation of the book.

Paul Kemp

◄2
2. Army gunners man a 40mm Bofors on board the merchant ship *Melbourne Star* during the 'Pedestal' operation. Although such weapons were intended for the defence of Malta and were therefore nominally part of the ship's cargo, they were used to augment the ship's AA armament. Air attacks developed from the afternoon of 11 August and increased in intensity the following day. (IWM A.11251)

▲ 3   ▼ 4

3. The island of Malta, strategically placed in the central Mediterranean and commanding the narrow channel between Sicily and North Africa. Captured by Britain in 1799, the island became the Royal Navy's principal base in the Mediterranean. Yet Malta was hideously vulnerable to blockade, since the island was not self-supporting and everything had to be brought in by sea. Italy's declaration of war on Britain and France in June 1940 placed the island in the forefront of the conflict. (IWM CM.4522)

4. Fairey IIIFs fly over units of the Mediterranean Fleet in Grand Harbour, Valetta (the island's capital city). For 150 years Malta had been a second home to the Royal Navy, yet the Admiralty had reluctantly to accept that the Mediterranean Fleet could not use the island as a base in time of war, since both the War Office and Air Ministry considered that, with Sicily only 60 miles away, it was indefensible. (IWM Q.99524)

5. Cant Z.1007 bombers over Valetta. Following the Italian declaration of war, the *Regia Aeronautica* launched the first of hundreds of air raids on 11 June 1940. The island was critically short of fighter aircraft, so 'Hurry', the first in a long series of operations whereby aircraft were flown there from aircraft carriers, took place between 31 July and 4 August 1940. Twelve Hurricanes and two Skuas were successfully flown off from the aircraft carrier HMS *Argus*. (IWM KY.7871C)

6. A heavily escorted Axis supply convoy under way to North Africa. Equally vulnerable to attack was the supply line to the Italian (and later German) army in North Africa. From the beginning, British light forces and submarines took a heavy toll of Axis supply ships, yet their very success only emphasized the threat that Malta-based forces posed to the Italian supply lines and, therefore, why the island had to be beaten into surrender. (IWM HU.5629)

5 ▲   **6 ▼**

▲7 ▼8

7. The cruiser HMS *Liverpool* at Alexandria after being torpedoed on 14 October while returning from covering Convoy MF.3 to Malta in Operation MB.6. *Liverpool* was attacked by aircraft south-east of Crete and sustained a hit forward which caused structural damage that was later compounded by the ignition of petrol vapour. The resulting explosion blew the roof off 'A' turret and severely damaged the fore end. She was taken in tow by HMS *Orion* and safely reached Alexandria on 16 October, but not before losing her bows en route. *Liverpool* had earlier taken part in Operation MB.5, a troop reinforcement convoy to Malta. (IWM FL.5701)

8. HMS *Ark Royal* leading *Argus* and *Renown* in Operation 'White' another aircraft ferry run to Malta in November 1940. Twelve Hurricanes and two Skuas were flown off from *Argus* but on this occasion eight Hurricanes and a Skua were lost on account of easterly winds and poor visibility over Malta. (IWM A.9543)

9. HMS *Illustrious* under attack on 10 January 1941 while providing distant cover during Operation 'Excess', a complicated operation involving the simultaneous passing of ships to Malta, Greece and Crete and the return of empty shipping from Malta. *Illustrious* was steaming north-west of Malta with the battleships *Warspite* (flagship of Admiral Cunningham) and *Valiant* and seven destroyers when, shortly after 12.30pm, the force was located by a large number of Ju 87 dive-bombers which pressed home their attack with great determination. *Illustrious* was often completely hidden by bomb splashes, and within ten minutes had been hit by six 1,000lb bombs which caused much damage. However, she managed to limp into Malta later that evening. This attack marked the first appearance of the Luftwaffe in the Mediterranean. (IWM ZZZ.328OD

10. *Illustrious* under attack in Grand Harbour: the ship is on the right of the photograph with the floating crane on her port side. Heroic efforts by her crew and the dockyard labour force enabled her to get away from Malta on 23 January and make for the safety of Alexandria at 24kts. Other casualties of Operation 'Excess' included the destroyer *Gallant*, mined on 10 January, and the cruiser *Southampton*, bombed and sunk on 11 January. (IWM MH.4624)

▲11   ▼12

11. HMS *Manchester*, a *Southampton* Class cruiser built in 1937, was one of the escorts for Convoy GM.1, consisting of six merchant ships; the escorts would also cover the return of six empty ships from Malta to Gibraltar, and the whole operation was codenamed 'Substance'. South of Sardinia, the convoy was subjected to severe air attacks, in which *Manchester* was badly damaged. (IWM HU.53148)

12. Seamen and soldiers, who were being carried to Malta as passengers in *Manchester*, place stores along the cruiser's starboard side to counteract the list after she had been bombed on 23 July 1941. A damage control party struggles to get by. (IWM A.4929)

13. The *Hunt* Class destroyer *Avonvale* comes alongside *Manchester*. *Avonvale* escorted the crippled cruiser back to Gibraltar. (IWM A.4950)

14. Another warship casualty of Operation 'Substance' was the destroyer HMS *Fearless*, seen here (right) badly on fire after being bombed on 23 July 1941. The destroyer on the left is *Forester*. The convoy reached Malta on 24 July without loss, although the freighter *Sydney Star* was damaged. (IWM A.4913)

13 ▲   14 ▼

 ▲ 15

15. A general view of Convoy WS.11X, Operation 'Halberd', in September 1941. This was a large, fast convoy which included ships bound for the Far East as well as Malta. The convoy left Gibraltar on 24 September and, during the five-day passage to Malta, was subjected to severe Axis air attacks. (IWM A.5647)
16. The convoy's cruiser escort under way. From left to right are HMS *Edinburgh*, HMS *Sheffield* and HMS *Kenya*. (IWM A.5645)
17. An Italian bomber flying through the intense anti-aircraft

barrage put up by the convoy's escorts. Heavy air attacks developed from 27 September onwards. (IWM A.5632)
18. HMS *Ark Royal* manoeuvring with ships of the convoy. The carrier's fighters proved of great value in breaking up air attacks away from the convoy. (IWM A.5628)
19. The wreckage of a Italian bomber in the water. Twelve Italian aircraft were claimed to have been shot down by AA fire or by fighters from *Ark Royal*. (IWM A.5640)

▼ 16

17 ▲

18 ▲   19 ▼

▲ 20   ▼ 21

20. The scale of the air attacks meant that sooner or later there would be casualties. HMS *Nelson* is shown down by the bows after being torpedoed by an Italian aircraft on 27 September. (IWM A.5641)

21. One of the convoy's freighters safely in Grand Harbour on 28 September. Only one merchant ship was lost, the 12,427grt *Imperial Star*, torpedoed by aircraft on 27 September. (IWM A.5769)

22. *Ark Royal* under way during Operation 'Perpetual', an aircraft ferrying operation to Malta also involving HMS *Argus* in November 1941. The two carriers were screened by the battleship *Malaya* and seven destroyers. Thirty-seven Hurricanes and seven Blenheims

were successfully flown off, although three of the Hurricanes failed to arrive. Hurricanes can be seen parked at the after end of *Ark Royal*'s flight deck. (IWM A.6318)

23. *Ark Royal* listing to starboard after being torpedoed by *U81* while on her way back to Gibraltar on 13 November 1941. The torpedo struck very deep on the starboard side abreast the starboard boiler room. Flooding spread and soon reached the middle and port boiler rooms via the smoke ducts, which had no baffles and were placed too low down in the ship. Electric power then failed because there were no diesel dynamos, and the order to abandon ship was given. (IWM A.6334)

24. The ship's company of *Ark Royal* leave the starboard side of the ship to board an escorting destroyer. Out of her complement of 1,580, only one man lost his life. (IWM A.6315)

25. The destroyer HMS *Legion* manoeuvres beside the sinking *Ark Royal*. Fourteen hours after the torpedo struck, the carrier finally sank within sight of Gibraltar. So often claimed as having been sunk by Goering's Luftwaffe, *Ark Royal* found that her luck had finally run out. (IWM A.6332)

26. Bombs falling astern of the cruiser HMS *Naiad* during the passage of the fast transport HMS *Breconshire*, visible astern of *Naiad* and heavily escorted by cruisers and destroyers, December 1941. (IWM A.7172)

27. An Italian bomber crashes into the sea during the attacks on *Breconshire* on 17 December 1941. On the same day the force was briefly threatened by two Italian battleships supported by light forces, but a stout defence, conducted by the escort, caused the Italians to break off the action. (IWM A.7173)

▲ 28   ▼ 29

28. The merchant ship *Glengyle* entering Grand Harbour in January 1942. *Glengyle* arrived at the island in Operation MF.2 and departed on 24 January in Operation MF.4. Convoy operations in the first two months of 1942 were characterized by the movement of small numbers or individual fast merchant ships under heavy escort. (IWM GM.349)

29. The merchant ship *Ajax* arriving on 19 January after the passage of Convoys MW.8A and MW.8B. *Ajax* was one of two ships in the slow Convoy MW.8A which left Alexandria on 16 January. On 17 January the destroyer *Gurkha* was torpedoed and sunk by *U133* and on the same day the other merchant ship, the

Thermopylae, was sunk in air attacks while returning to Alexandria after engine problems. (IWM 7348)

30. The fast portion of the convoy, MW.8B, was more fortunate. Consisting of the *Clan Ferguson* and the *City of Calcutta*, it reached Malta without loss, although delayed by bad weather. The photograph shows *Clan Ferguson* at Malta on 19 January. (IWM A.7353)

31. The commissioned auxiliary supply ship HMS *Breconshire*, which had been brought out of Malta on 6 January in Operation MF.2 and returned to the island on 24 January in Operation MF.4.

▲ 32

32. The *Clan Chattan* burning after being bombed on 14 February 1942 during the passage of Convoy MW.9A. The convoy consisted of three merchant ships, none of which reached Malta. *Clan Campbell* was bombed on 13 February and escorted into Tobruk, whence she later returned to Alexandria, and *Rowallan Castle* had to be sunk on the same day after being badly damaged. (IWM AD No. 8061)

33. A view from the after end of the aircraft carrier *Eagle*'s island during Operation 'Spotter' in March 1942: the carrier *Argus* is leading the cruiser *Hermione*. 'Spotter' was an aircraft ferrying operation in which fifteen Spitfires and seven Blenheims were

successfully flown off on during the night of 5–6 March and was the first such voyage since the loss of *Ark Royal*. A similar operation, codenamed 'Picket', was mounted at the end of March. (IWM A.9584)

34. Malta would need every aircraft available. This is an aerial reconnaissance photograph of the airfield at Castelvetrano on Sicily taken in early 1942. Between seventy and eighty aircraft can be seen on the field, most of them Z.1007 and SM.79 torpedo-bombers; others are transports, including Ju 52s of the Luftwaffe's *Fliegerkorps II*, which was transferred from the Russian Front early in 1942 to spearhead the air offensive against Malta. (IWM C.4183)

▼ 33

34 ▶

▲35   ▼36

35. Convoy MW.10, consisting of the merchant ships *Pampas*, *Talabot* and *Clan Campbell* and the commissioned auxiliary supply ship *Breconshire*, and escorted by the cruisers *Cleopatra* (flying the flag of Rear-Admiral Philip Vian), *Dido* and *Euryalus* and every destroyer available; the cruiser *Penelope* and destroyer *Legion* would meet the convoy west of Crete. In an apparent reversal of their prewar position, the Chiefs of Staff had decided that the maintenance of offensive forces on Malta was so important that the most drastic steps were justified to fight the convoy through to the island. (IWM A.8162)

36. Rear-Admiral Philip Vian (left), in command of the escort. An aggressive fighting officer, he was determined to see the four merchant ships through to Malta even if 'enemy surface forces make contact'. (IWM A.17969)

37. The Italian battleship *Littorio*, which sortied from Taranto with two 8in and four 6in gunned cruisers on the night of 21–22 March to attack the convoy. By 4.40pm on 22 March, this formidable force was in contact with the convoy in the Gulf of Sirte and the stage was set for the Second Battle of Sirte – one of the most skilfully conducted convoy defence actions of the Second World War. The photograph of *Littorio* was taken after the Italian surrender in 1943. (IWM AX.7A)

38. HMS *Euryalus* fires her six forward 5.25in guns at the Italian ships. The smokescreen also served as a barrier, from behind which Vian's cruisers and destroyers would emerge to launch torpedo and gun attacks on the *Littorio* and her consorts, all the while striving to keep the Italians away from the convoy. (IWM A.8160)

◄**38**

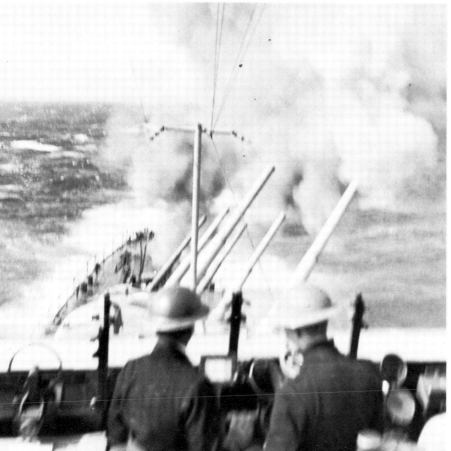

▲39   ▼40

39. HMS *Kipling* emerges from the smokescreen to fire torpedoes in an attack launched at 6.41pm with *Jervis*, *Kelvin*, *Kingston* and *Legion*. Twenty-five torpedoes were fired by the five destroyers, one of which struck *Littorio* on her starboard side, causing her to break off the action. The battle was over: four weak cruisers and eleven destroyers had held at bay a capital ship and six cruisers in rough weather for nearly two and a half hours. (IWM A.8165)

40. HMS *Kingston* received a hit from a 15in shell during the torpedo attack but reached Malta safely. While under repair at Malta, however, she was bombed and became a constructive total loss, as seen in the photograph. (IWM A.9636)

▲ 41

41. An Axis aircraft flies through the barrage put up by the escorts. While the cruisers and destroyers were beating off the Italian task force, the convoy's close escort had to contend with severe air attacks mounted by German and Italian aircraft. Generally the aircraft were kept at bay, although the air battles in heavy weather were a great test of the endurance and skill of the British defenders. (IWM A.8167)

42. HMS *Breconshire*, veteran of a number of Malta convoys, disabled and on fire after an air attack on 23 March in the final approach to Malta. At 1900hrs on 22 March, the four merchant ships had dispersed to enter Malta independently, each with two escorts. In the original plan it was intended that the ships arrive at Malta just after daybreak on 23 March, but the action with the Italian fleet had forced the convoy south of its route, thus giving the Luftwaffe a second chance. Early on the morning of 23 March air attacks commenced again, despite the heavy weather, and the ships had to run the gauntlet all the way into Grand Harbour with their

escorts now desperately short of ammunition. (IWM AX.115A)

43. HMS *Penelope* attempted to take the stricken *Breconshire* in tow, but the great draught of the ship, together with the heavy seas, made it impossible. She was anchored and, on 25 March, successfully towed into Marsaxlokk, but sank on 27 March after further air attacks. Other casualties of the final approach to Malta were the *Clan Campbell*, bombed from a height of just 50ft while only twenty miles away from Grand Harbour, and the destroyer *Southwold*, mined on 24 March while standing by *Breconshire* outside Grand Harbour. (IWM AX.112A)

44. One of the two surviving merchant ships, the *Pampas*, on fire at Malta after being bombed on 26 March. All but two of her holds were flooded. The other survivor, the *Talabot*, was also bombed on the 26th and had to be sunk lest her cargo of ammunition explode. Only 5,000 tons of the 26,000 tons of cargo carried in the four ships of MW.10 were safely landed. (IWM A.9499)

▼ 42

43 ▲   44 ▼

▲45   ▼46

45. The arrival of the convoy marked the beginning of an all-out assault by the Luftwaffe on Malta. Between 24 March and 12 April there were 2,159 bomber sorties against the island, and an estimated 1,870 tons of bombs were dropped. Here, Valetta's AA defences are in action during a night raid. (IWM GM.1766)

46. Devastation in Valetta's naval dockyard caused by the April air raids. In the background are the remains of the destroyer *Lance*. On 5 April, while in dry dock, *Lance*'s side was blown in by a bomb which exploded in the dock, causing it to flood. In all, nine Allied warships were sunk or damaged at Malta during the April raids. (IWM A.9634)

47. Submarines at Malta in December 1941. Under the strain of the Axis air offensive, it became impossible to operate submarines and surface ships from the island and accordingly, on 26 April, the 10th Submarine Flotilla was ordered to move to Alexandria. This move meant the temporary cessation of the submarine offensive against Axis shipping. (IWM A.6929)

48. The cruiser HMS *Penelope*, built in 1935 by Harland and Wolff, had been badly damaged in the March convoy and was at risk from further damage if she remained at Malta. She therefore sailed independently from Gibraltar on 8 April 1942 and arrived safely on the 10th, having endured many air attacks en route. (IWM A.7352)

▲ 49   ▼ 50

49. A view of *Penelope*'s starboard side abreast 'B' turret and the bridge, showing the plating covered in splinters from Axis air attacks which earned the ship the nickname 'HMS Pepperpot'. (IWM A.8602)

50. The Admiralty decided that it was impossible to send another convoy to Malta in April or May 1942 because of the losses suffered during March and because of the demands on shipping from other theatres of operations. However, Malta was not entirely forgotten. The photo shows the US aircraft carrier *Wasp*, which participated in two ferry operations to Malta, 'Calendar' in April 1942 and 'Bowery' in May 1942, in which a total of 113 Spitfires were flown off. The effect of these reinforcements on Malta's air defence was near-miraculous: the island's war diary reported that 'daylight raiding was brought to an abrupt end'. (IWM A.9231)

51. Convoy WS.19S under attack during the voyage from Gibraltar to Malta in June 1942. By June, Malta's supply position was critical and the Admiralty resolved to send two convoys: one, codenamed WS.19S, Operation 'Harpoon', would sail eastbound from Gibraltar whilst the other would sail westbound from the Middle East. The eastbound convoy consisited of five merchant ships and a tanker, the *Kentucky*, the latter visible on the right in this photograph. (IWM A.10177)

52. The battleship HMS *Malaya* under air attack. The convoy's escort was woefully weak and consisted of *Malaya*, the carriers *Eagle* and *Argus*, three cruisers and three destroyers, but on reaching the Sicilian Narrows on the evening of 14 June this force turned back to Gibraltar while the convoy carried on to Malta with the close escort of one old cruiser, *Cairo*, nine destroyers and four minesweepers. (IWM A.10185)

53. Smoke rises from a crashed enemy aircraft. In the four days that the convoy took to reach Malta, thirteen Axis aircraft were shot down by the fighters from *Argus* and *Eagle*, while another sixteen were destroyed by AA gunfire from the escorts. (IWM A.10200)

54. The Italian cruiser *Eugenio di Savoia*, which led a force of two cruisers and five destroyers to attack the convoy. The Italians had left Cagliari on 14 June and by 6.20am were in contact with the convoy. This photograph was taken on 11 September 1943 after *Savoia* had surrendered at Malta. (IWM NA.6572)

55. The fleet destroyers of the close escort move out in line ahead to engage the Italians, making a smokescreen to hide the merchant ships. Even though the destroyers' 4.7in guns were far outranged by the Italians' heavier armament, they still fired rounds 'for moral effect'. A well-directed defensive action drove the Italians away, but the attack had delayed the convoy. (IWM FLM.1091)

56. The cruiser HMS *Cairo* at Malta after the arrival of the convoy on 16 June. While *Cairo* had been directing the defence against the Italian cruisers, a strong force of Ju 87 dive-bombers had attacked the convoy. Deprived of *Cairo*'s air direction facility and of the destroyers' firepower, the merchant ships were easy game for the Stukas: the *Chant* was sunk and the *Kentucky* and *Burdwan* so badly damaged that they later had to be sunk. Since the *Tanimbar* had been torpedoed by an aircraft on 14 June, only two merchant ships out of the six remained afloat. (IWM A.10413)

▲53 ▼54

55▲

56▲ 57▼

57. The destroyer *Bedouin* sinking on 15 June 1942. *Bedouin* was severely damaged in the engagement with the Italian ships and was later taken in tow by HMS *Partridge*, but while trying to rejoin the convoy the two destroyers were attacked by the Italian cruisers. *Partridge* gallantly slipped the tow and attempted to draw the cruisers' fire, but in a subsequent air attack *Bedouin* was torpedoed and sunk, although not before she had shot down her assailant. (IWM HU.2278)

▲58   ▼59

58. Damage to HMS *Partridge*. After the loss of *Bedouin*, *Partridge* was shelled by the Italian cruisers and then bombed by four German aircraft. Her helm was jammed hard over and it took more than an hour to get it amidships; during that time she had to lie stopped, watching the Italian warships rescue *Bedouin*'s survivors. When able to get under way, *Partridge* proceeded to Gibraltar, where she arrived on 17 June. (IWM A.10365)

59. The Polish destroyer *Kujawiak*, which was mined during the approach to Malta on 16 June and later had to be sunk. Owing to confusion over times of arrival, the convoy and escort reached the minefields outside Malta before the minesweepers, which ought to have been sweeping ahead of them. (IWM FL.804)

60. The destroyer HMS *Badsworth*, another casualty of the minefields outside Malta, being assisted to her moorings in Grand Harbour. Other casualties included the destroyer *Matchless*, the minesweeper *Hebe* and the merchant ship *Orari*, all of which reached Malta safely. (IWM A.10411)

61. The merchant ship *Troilus*, the only member of the convoy to reach Malta undamaged, in No. 5 dock. Lighters lie alongside the ship to take off supplies. (IWM GM.1095)

▲62 ▼63

62. The damaged *Orari*, her list to port caused by a mine, being unloaded at Malta. British servicemen and Maltese dockers unloaded 3,000 tons of supplies from the two ships within twenty-four hours. (IWM A.10417)

63. A view of the *Orari*'s side, showing the mine damage. After a patch had been placed over the hole, this ship, together with *Troilus* and the destroyers *Matchless* and *Badsworth*, was brought safely back to Gibraltar in Operation 'Ascendant' in August 1942. (IWM A.10430)

64. A general view of the westbound convoy MW.11, codenamed 'Vigorous', which sailed in two parts from Port Said and Haifa and consisted of seven heavily escorted merchant ships. On the right of the picture is the disarmed battleship HMS *Centurion*, which acted as an AA ship. (IWM A.10470)

65. The submarine HMS *Triton*, which landed commandos on the island of Crete on the night of 13–14 June to attack enemy airfields. Twenty-eight aircraft, six lorries and 12,500 gallons of petrol were destroyed as a result of this raid, but it had little impact in terms of the massive air assault to which the convoy was subjected. (IWM HU.51)

66. A pillar of smoke marks the end of the *Hunt* Class destroyer *Airedale* after attacks by over a dozen aircraft on 15 June. The ship was completely disabled and had to be scuttled. (IWM A.10473)

▲ 67   ▼ 68

67. Damage to the bows of the cruiser *Newcastle*, torpedoed by an Italian MTB from 500yds off the bow early in the morning of 15 June. The MTB was sighted early enough for one torpedo to be avoided, but the second struck well forward. Efficient damage control enabled *Newcastle* to make 24kts, but while she was steaming up to rejoin the convoy another MTB torpedo attack caused the loss of the destroyer *Hasty*. (IWM HU.51289)

68. The Italian battleship *Vittorio Veneto* which, together with her sister-ship *Littorio* and escorted by four cruisers and eleven destroyers, sailed from Taranto on the night of 14 June to attack the convoy. This powerful force did not have events their own way. Aircraft from Malta and Egypt continually attacked the Italians, but although these attacks were pressed home with great bravery, only one bomb struck *Littorio* on the morning of the 15th. Later that day, when the Italians had given up their attempt to find the convoy, *Littorio* was damaged again, this time by a torpedo dropped by a

Wellington from Malta. (IWM A.19481)

69. The Italian cruiser *Trento*, one of the four cruisers in the Italian force. *Trento* was successfully bombed by Beauforts from Malta on 15 June and later sunk by torpedo by the submarine HMS *Umbra*. (IWM HU.52347)

70. HMS *Cleopatra*, flagship of Vice-Admiral Vian, beating off an air attack. Although the Italian fleet was never nearer than 100 miles to the convoy, it succeeded in stopping the ships getting through to Malta. The convoy had lost valuable time in manoeuvring to avoid the Italian fleet and, in the meantime, had been subjected to heavy air and MTB attacks. Ammunition stocks were falling as low as 30 per cent in some ships, and so it was with the greatest reluctance that, on the evening of 15 June, Admiral Harwood, CinC Eastern Mediterranean, ordered Vian to return to Alexandria and abandon the attempt to fight his way through. (IWM A.10478)

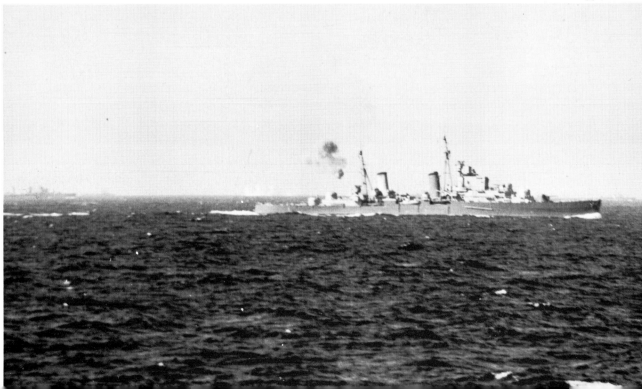

▲71 ▼72

71. The cruiser HMS *Hermione*, which was torpedoed on 16 June by *U205* while returning to Alexandria. British warships losses in Operation 'Vigorous' amounted to one cruiser and three destroyers sunk and another five damaged. One merchant ship, the *Bhutan*, was bombed and sunk on 14 June and another, the *Aagtekirk*, had to put into Tobruk, where she was later bombed and sunk. Italian and German losses were estimated to be 21 aircraft shot down. (IWM A.5742)

72. The minelayer HMS *Welshman*, built in 1940 by Hawthorn Leslie, was able to use her phenomenally high speed of 36kts to sail independently from Gibraltar to Malta carrying important supplies, and from 1 May to 24 July 1942 she made three round trips. The photograph shows her arriving at Malta on her second trip on 15 June 1942, having proceeded at high speed ahead of the 'Harpoon' convoy. Note the false caps added to the funnels and the false break in the forecastle, intended to disguise her as a Vichy French *Leopard* Class destroyer. (IWM A.10419)

73. Only hours after arriving at Malta and having discharged her cargo, *Welshman* heads back to sea for the high-speed passage to Gibraltar, followed by the cruiser *Cairo*. (IWM A.10415)

74. *Welshman* passes through the boom in Grand Harbour on 16 July 1942 on her third voyage to the island. The French disguise has been removed. (IWM GM.1369)

▲75   ▼76

75. *Welshman* lies alongside No. 5 dock while her supplies are unloaded. The minelayer was deliberately listed to port to give Axis air reconnaissance the impression that she had been damaged. (IWM A.10839)

76. Working parties unload supplies from *Welshman*'s mine doors at the stern on to the jetty, using a lighter as a pontoon. The vessel's capacious mine deck provided an ideal storage area. (IWM A.10841)

77. Her supplies unloaded, *Welshman* heads back to sea on 16 July 1942, passing the wreck of the destroyer HMS *Gallant* in the foreground. (IWM A.11128)

78. Maltese workmen remove grain from one of the island's many underground granaries. Although the supplies brought in by *Welshman* and the 'Harpoon' operation eased the situation, the island desperately needed another convoy, but the lack of carrier-borne fighter aircraft meant that none would sail until August, so the Maltese had to 'tighten their belts' even further. The summer of 1942 marked the nadir of Britain's efforts to keep Malta supplied. With the Axis apparently triumphant throughout the world, the fate of the island depended upon the successful arrival of the August convoy. (IWM BM.12411)

77▲   78▼

▲ 79   ▼ 80

79. Rear-Admiral Harold Burrough shakes hands with Captain Dudley Mason, the master of the tanker *Ohio*, after a conference on board Burrough's flagship, HMS *Nigeria*, which preceded the sailing of convoy WS.21S to Malta in August 1942. Codenamed Operation 'Pedestal', WS.21S consisted of thirteen merchant ships and a tanker and was escorted by the largest number of warships ever employed for a single convoy. Burrough was in command of the portion of escort known as Force X, consisting of four cruisers and eleven destroyers which would accompany the convoy all the way to Malta. (IWM A.11249)

80. The battleship HMS *Nelson*, flagship of Vice-Admiral Neville Syfret, commanding the portion of the escort known as Force Z, which comprised two battleships, four aircraft carriers, three cruisers and fifteen destroyers and would escort the convoy as far as the Sicilian Narrows and then return to Gibraltar. The photograph shows *Nelson* at Portsmouth in 1937. (IWM DS.395/13)

81. Operation 'Beserk', 5 August 1942. The convoy sailed from the Clyde on 3 August, and while on passage to Gibraltar the merchant ships practised station-keeping and the carriers high-speed manoeuvres. Here HMS *Indomitable* leads HMS *Argus* round in a turn to starboard. The old carrier *Argus* was included in the operation for the purposes of 'Beserk' only. (IWM A.11158)

▲82

82. A general view of 'Pedestal' under way. The convoy passed through the Straits of Gibraltar on the night of 9–10 August. On the right of the photograph is the old aircraft carrier *Furious*, which successfully flew off 38 Spitfires to Malta on 11 August in Operation 'Bellows' before returning to Gibraltar. On 12 August, during the return voyage, her escort, the destroyer *Wolverine*, rammed and sank the Italian submarine *Dagabur*. (IWM A.11149)

83. The aircraft carrier *Eagle* almost on her beam ends after being torpedoed by *U73*, which had been able to penetrate the destroyer screen while some of the escorts were away refuelling from the oiler. At the same time asdic conditions were poor because of the disturbance in the water created by the wakes of the destroyers proceeding at high speed to and from the oiler. (IWM A.11302)

▼83

84. An Italian aircraft flies over the convoy in the air attacks which were such a feature of the 'Pedestal' convoy. (IWM HU.43445)

85. A destroyer, possibly HMS *Bramham*, stands by the freighter *Deucalion* after she had been bombed on 12 August. The merchantman had to leave the convoy, was later torpedoed by a German aircraft and had to be sunk by *Bramham*. (IWM A.11188)

86. The Italian submarine *Cobalto* passing down the starboard side of the destroyer HMS *Ithuriel* after having been rammed. On the evening of 12 August the convoy passed through an area in which a number of Italian submarines were concentrated. *Cobalto* was depth-charged to the surface by HMS *Pathfinder* and rammed by *Ithuriel*. (IWM AP.13356C)

84 ▲

85 ▲   86 ▼

▲87

87. The destroyer HMS *Foresight* sinking on 13 August. The ship was a casualty of the fierce air attacks which developed in the evening of 12 August and was disabled by an aerial torpedo. She was taken in tow by HMS *Tartar* but had to be sunk the next day. (IWM HU.47957)

89. HMS *Indomitable*, another casualty of the air attacks of the evening of 12 August, on fire after being struck by three bombs which put the flight deck out of action and started severe fires. Excellent damage control, however, meant that by 9.15pm the carrier was under way again, although at reduced speed. Later that evening, as the convoy approached the Sicilian Narrows, the battleships, carriers and destroyers of Force Z withdrew, leaving the merchant ships and Force X to carry on to Malta. (IWM A.15964)

▼88

89. A torpedo fired by the Italian submarine *Axum* strikes the tanker *Ohio* on her port side in an attack launched on the evening of 12 August. After the withdrawal of Force Z the convoy changed formation to pass through the narrow Skerki Channel and, in doing so, the ships lost formation and became bunched up. At this critical moment, *Axum* penetrated the screen and fired a salvo of four torpedoes, one of which struck the *Ohio*, another Admiral Burrough's flagship *Nigeria* and the third and fourth the cruiser *Cairo*. It was a bad evening for the convoy, for in further air attacks the merchant ships *Clan Ferguson* and *Empire Hope* were sunk. (IWM HU.47560)

90. The crew of a multiple pom-pom gun on board HMS *Manchester*. The litter of empty cartridge cases on the deck testifies to the ferocity of the air attacks. (IWM A.11180)

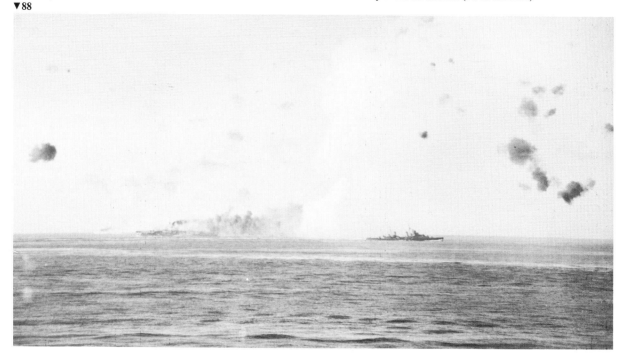

89▲ 90▼

▲91

91. An Italian MAS boat of the type which successfully attacked the convoy as it rounded Cape Bon early in the morning of 13 August. The merchant ships had not yet regained formation after the attacks of the previous evening and was thus particularly vulnerable to this form of attack. (IWM HU.43228)

92. A *Dido* Class cruiser, possibly HMS *Charybdis*, firing against MAS boats during the night of 12–13 August. *Charybdis*, together with destroyers *Eskimo* and *Tartar*, had been ordered by Admiral Syfret to rejoin the convoy to replace *Cairo* and the damaged *Nigeria*. (IWM A.11247)

93. HMS *Manchester*, the principal casualty of the MAS boat attacks. She was disabled and later had to be sunk, the survivors becoming prisoners of the Vichy French regime in North Africa. The photograph shows *Manchester* at Portsmouth on 2 May 1942, after repairs to damage sustained in the 'Substance' convoy had been completed. (IWM FL.4156)

94. A merchant ship abandoned and on fire on the morning of 13 August. MAS boat attacks accounted for the loss of the merchant ships *Almeria Lykes*, *Santa Elisa*, *Wairangi* and *Glenorchy*. (IWM HU.43464)

▼92

▲95 ▼96

95. A German dive-bomber crashes in flames after being shot down by the AA fire of the escorts. From the morning of 13 August fierce air attacks developed. (IWM A.11172)

96. The merchant ship *Wairmarama* explodes after being bombed on 13 August. The ship was attacked by two Ju 87 dive-bombers, the immediate explosion destroying one of her attackers. (IWM HU.43689)

97. An aerial torpedo caught in the paravane of the merchant ship *Port Chalmers*. The ship could not reduce speed to free the torpedo for fear that it would explode against the ship's side, and in the end the whole paravane fitting was ditched and the torpedo exploded harmlessly on the bottom. (IWM HU.1966)

98. The merchant ship *Dorset* under attack on 13 August. *Dorset* survived repeated air attacks but was eventually sunk that evening. (IWM A.11173)

99. The Italian cruiser *Muzio Attendolo* at Naples after losing her bows to a torpedo fired by HMS/M *Unbroken* on 13 August off Stromboli. *Attendolo*, together with *Bolzano*, had left port in southern Italy on 11 and 12 August but had been ordered to return to harbour after a successful deception operation mounted by the RAF convinced the *Supamarina* that superior British forces were at sea. It was on their return voyage that the cruisers were attacked by *Unbroken*, which also damaged *Bolzano* in the same attack. This was the only occasion on which the 'Pedestal' convoy was threatened by the Italian fleet. (IWM HU.2288)

97 ▲

98 ▲   99 ▼

▲100　　▼101

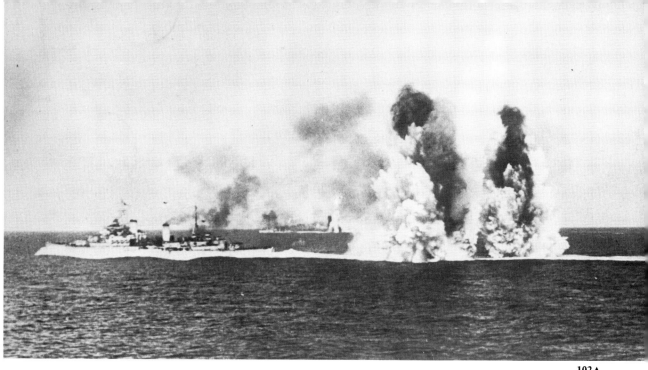

100. The *Melbourne Star* enters Grand Harbour, Malta, on the afternoon of 13 August as one of the five surviving merchant ships to reach the island. (IWM GM.1429)
101. The merchant ship *Port Chalmers*, one of the survivors of the 'Pedestal' convoy, arrives at Malta on 13 August 1942 cheered in to her moorings by servicemen and civilians. (IWM GM.1426)
102. The cruiser *Kenya* under attack in August 1942 during the return of the ships of Force X to Gibraltar. They parted from the

convoy on the 13th and made a fast passage back to Gibraltar, enduring attacks by aircraft, submarines and MAS boats en route. (IWM HU.53130)
103. The merchantman *Rochester Castle* proceeds to her berth in Grand Harbour. She had been damaged by a MAS boat on 13 August and again in subsequent air attacks, but had safely reached port. (IWM GM.1430)

▲ 104　　▼105

104. *Brisbane Star* was another of the survivors. Torpedoed and severely damaged on 12 August, she had proceeded independently to Malta, where she arrived on 15 August, having avoided the attentions of German, Italian and Vichy French forces. (IWM GM.1436)

105. Damage to the starboard side of the stem of *Brisbane Star* sustained on the night of 12–13 August. (IWM GM.1451)

106. The real heroine of the 'Pedestal' convoy was the tanker *Ohio*, seen here with the destroyer HMS *Penn* alongside. Torpedoed on 12 August, she was disabled by near-misses in air attacks on the 13th in which a German aircraft crashed on her upper deck after releasing its bomb. (IWM A.11262/GM.1469)

107. Since the tanker could not steam under her own power she was taken in tow by *Ledbury* and *Penn*, but the two destroyers found the big tanker impossible to manoeuvre. *Penn* thus went alongside *Ohio*'s starboard side while *Ledbury* was secured to the tanker's port side, and between them the two warships brought the crippled tanker slowly towards Malta. (IWM GM.1505)

107▼

▲108

108. Screened by the guns of an escorting warship, *Ohio* is brought slowly towards Grand Harbour on the morning of 15 August. HMS *Ledbury* is still secured to *Ohio*'s port side, while a dockyard tug manoeuvres astern. The safe arrival of the *Ohio* represented a magnificent feat of seamanship by her master, her crew and the men of the escorting warships. (IWM A.11261)

109. Now under the control of dockyard tugs, although with *Ledbury* still secured to her port side, *Ohio* moves up Grand Harbour to a tumultuous welcome. The cost of 'Pedestal' had been high – an aircraft carrier, two cruisers and a destroyer sunk, together with a further three warships damaged and nine merchant ships lost. (IWM GM.1481)

▼109

110. Operation 'Ceres'. Once the ships were safely at their moorings, the work of unloading some 32,000 tons of cargo began. The greater part of the garrison and the entire dockyard workforce was mobilized to complete this work as quickly as possible, in case Axis aircraft attacked and sank the ships at their moorings. In the event, Malta was left unmolested and the work proceeded uninterrupted. Here, sacks of flour are unloaded from the hold of one of the merchant ships. (IWM GM.1448)

111. The minelayer HMS *Manxman*, which sailed from Port Said on 10 November 1942 for Malta with a cargo of 350 tons of food and 200 personnel. She arrived on 12 November, the first ship to visit the island since the 'Pedestal' convoy. (IWM A.6042)

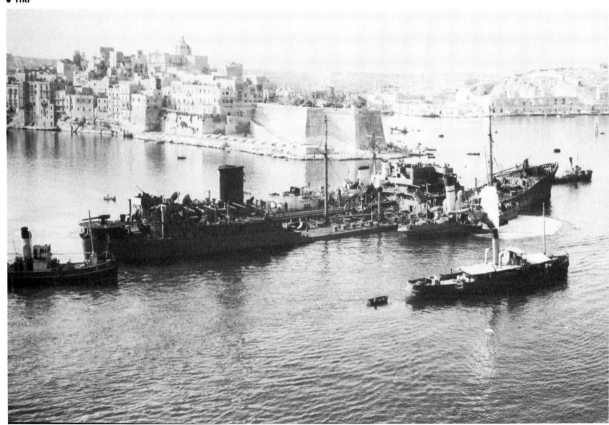

110 ▲ 111 ▼

▲112

112. The crowded scene on *Manxman's* mine deck, packed with stores and personnel on passage to Malta. On 1 December, on her return journey to Gibraltar, the minelayer was torpedoed and badly damaged by *U375*. (IWM A.13025)

113. HMS *Pandora*, which together with HMS *Proteus* made the first of many submarine supply runs to Malta in August 1940 in Operation 'Tube'. This service became known as the 'Magic Carpet'. *Pandora* made several voyages to Malta carrying supplies and RAF personnel, but after arriving on the island on 31 March 1942 she was bombed and sunk before her cargo could be unloaded.

114. HMS *Olympus*, an 'O' Class submarine built in 1928, refuels in

Manoel Creek, December 1941. *Olympus, Clyde, Rorqual* and *Parthian* were among the most successful submarines to run the blockade from June 1941 to October 1942. *Olympus* was mined with heavy loss of life while evacuating submarine personnel from Malta in May 1942. (IWM A.6938)

115. A section of the casing of the submarine HMS *Clyde*, photographed at Gibraltar in between 'Magic Carpet' runs to Malta. The canisters on top of the casing are for carrying spare torpedoes for use by the submarines based at Malta. From July to December 1941 sixteen stores trips were made – roughly one every twelve days. (IWM MH.30017)

▼ 113

▲116

▲117 ▼118

116. HMS *Rorqual*, a submarine minelayer built in 1936. On one voyage from Alexandria *Rorqual* carried 24 personnel, 147 bags of mail, two tons of medical stores, 62 tons of aviation spirit and 45 tons of kerosene. Carrying aviation spirit in external fuel tanks posed special problems: the smell of petrol on the bridge was so strong that pyrotechnic recognition signals had to be forbidden. (IWM A.14883)

117. Members of the ship's company of HMS *Porpoise* display a special 'Jolly Roger' commemorating 'Magic Carpet' operations to Malta. The flag records nine such voyages to Malta, and the letters PCS stand for 'Porpoise Carrier Service'. (IWM A.14006)

118. A view from the bridge of *Euryalus* as she escorts a convoy of four merchant ships to Malta in an Operation codenamed 'Stoneage', November 1942. The four ships left Alexandria on the 16th, arriving at Malta during the night of 19th–20th without incident. (IWM A.13677)

119. Unloading the 'Stoneage' ships at night with the aid of floodlights. A further convoy in December, MW.14, gave the island enough supplies to last until the middle of 1943. The siege of Malta was over. (IWM GM.1932)

120. Malta's triumph. 'Be pleased to inform their Lordships that the Italian battle fleet now lies at anchor under guns of the fortress of Malta' was the signal sent by Admiral Cunningham to mark the surrender of the Italian fleet on 11 September 1943. It was fitting that the surrender should have taken place at Malta, the island which had endured so much and which had played such a vital part in the Mediterranean campaign. (IWM NA.6592)

WARBIRDS ILLUSTRATED

13. Military Helicopters by Michael J. Gething
24. US Spyplanes by Eric Simonsen
25. RAF Air Power Today by Michael J. Gething and Lindsay T. Peacock
27. F-4 Phantom Vol. 1 by Robert C. Stern
28. World Fighters 1955-1985 by Michael J. H. Taylor
29. USAF Today by Dana Bell
30. Strategic Bombers 1945-1985 by Michael J. H. Taylor
31. Air War over Germany: The USAAF Bombing Campaign 1944-1945 by Jeffrey L. Ethell
32. Mirage by Jean-Pierre Decock
34. US Naval and Marine Aircraft Today by Don Linn
38. US Army Air Forces World War Two Vol. 1 by Jeffrey L. Ethell
40. Fairchild Republic A-10 by Dana Bell
41. Boeing B-17 Flying Fortress by Jeffrey L. Ethell
42. Tornado by Michael J. Gething
43. Junkers Bombers Vol. 1 by Manfred Griehl
44. F-104 Starfighter by Peter R. Foster
45. Argentine Air Forces in the Falklands Conflict by Salvador Mafe Huertas and Jesus Romero Briasco
46. F-4 Phantom Vol. 2 by Robert C. Stern
47. Army Gunships in Vietnam by Bob Chenoweth
48. Soviet Air Power Today by Michael J. Gething
49. F-105 Thunderchief by Robert F. Dorr
50. Fifty Classic Warbirds by Jeffrey L. Ethell
51. Canberra and B-57 by Ken Delve
52. German Jets of World War Two by Manfred Griehl

VINTAGE WARBIRDS

1. The Royal Flying Corps in World War One by Raymond L. Rimell
2. The German Army Air Service in World War One by Raymond L. Rimell
3. RAF between the Wars by Raymond L. Rimell
4. The Bristol Fighter by J. M. Bruce
6. Fokker Fighters of World War One by Alex Imrie
7. Air War over Great Britain 1914-1918 by Raymond L. Rimell
8. German Air Aces of World War One by Alex Imrie

9. World War One in the Air by Raymond L. Rimell
10. Nieuport Aircraft of World War One by J. M. Bruce

WARSHIPS ILLUSTRATED

1. The Royal Navy in the 1980s Vol. 1 by Paul Beaver
2. The US Navy Today Vol. 1 by Norman Polmar
3. NATO Navies of the 1980s by Paul Beaver
4. British Destroyers in World War Two by R. A. Burt
5. Nuclear Powered Submarines by Paul Beaver
6. Soviet Navy Today by Milan Vego
7. British Destroyers in World War One by R. A. Burt
8. The World's Aircraft Carriers 1914-1945 by Roger Chesneau
9. The Russian Convoys 1941-1945 by Paul J. Kemp
10. The US Navy in World War Two 1941-1942 by Robert C. Stern
11. British Submarines in World War Two by Paul J. Kemp
12. British Cruisers in World War One by R. A. Burt
13. U-Boats of World War Two by Robert C. Stern
14. Malta Convoys by Paul J. Kemp

TANKS ILLUSTRATED

1. Allied Forces Central Europe by Pierre Touzin
3. Israeli Tanks and Combat Vehicles by Steven J. Zaloga
5. British Battle Tanks 1945 to the Present by Simon Dunstan
6. Tank War Vietnam by Simon Dunstan
9. Last of the Panzers: German Tanks 1944-1945 by William Auerbach
10. D-Day Tank Battles: Beachhead to Breakout by George Balin
11. Patton's Tanks by Steven J. Zaloga
12. British Army Fighting Vehicles 1945 to the Present by Simon Dunstan
13. US Infantry Combat Vehicles Today by Steven J. Zaloga and Michael Green
14. Tank War Korea by Simon Dunstan
15. US Halftracks of World War Two by Steven J. Zaloga
16. Operation Barbarossa by Steven J. Zaloga and James Grandsen
17. Afrika Korps by George Balin

18. Self-Propelled Howitzers by Simon Dunstan
19. US Tank Destroyers of World War Two by Steven J. Zaloga
20. Allied Tanks North Italy, World War Two by Bryan Perrett
21. Allied Tanks North Africa, World War Two by Brian Perrett
22. Scorpion: The CVR(T) Range by Simon Dunstan
23. British Combat Vehicles Today by Simon Dunstan
24. Modern Israeli Tanks and Combat Vehicles by Samuel M. Katz
25. The Churchill Tank by Chris Ellis
26. US Mechanized Firepower Today by Steven J. Zaloga
27. Hitler's Panzers: The Years of Aggression by Brian Perrett
28. Panzer Armee Afrika: Tripoli to Tunis by Peter Gudgin
29. US Marine Tanks in World War Two by Steven J. Zaloga

UNIFORMS ILLUSTRATED

1. US Special Forces of World War Two by Leroy Thompson
3. US Special Forces 1945 to the Present by Leroy Thompson
4. The British Army in Northern Ireland by Simon Dunstan
8. Soviet Army Uniforms Today by Steven J. Zaloga
9. Soviet Army Uniforms in World War Two by Steven J. Zaloga
10. The Paras: The British Parachute Regiment by James G. Shortt
11. US Marines in World War Two by Robert C. Stern
12. Israeli Defence Forces 1948 to the Present by Lee Russell and Sam Katz
13. British Special Forces 1945 to the Present by James G. Shortt
14. US Army Uniforms Europe 1944-1945 by Cameron P. Laughlin and John P. Langellier
15. The French Foreign Legion 1940 to the Present by Yves L. Cadiou and Tibor Szecsko
16. Modern American Soldier by Lee Russell and Arnold Meisner
17. Israeli Elite Units by Samuel M. Katz
18. US Airborne Forces of World War Two by Cameron P. Laughlin
19. The Boer War by Philip J. Haythornthwaite
20. The Commandos, World War Two to the Present by Derek Oakley
21. Victorian Colonial Wars by Philip J. Haythornthwaite

For an illustrated catalogue describing these and other books published by Arms & Armour Press, or if you wish to receive further information about specific subjects, please write to the address given on the back cover of this book, identifying your areas of interest.